REBECCA ST. JAMES

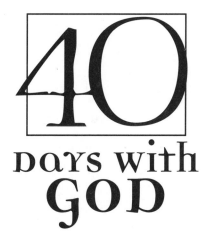

40

days with GOD

REBECCA ST. JAMES

40

DAYS with GOD

A DEVOTIONAL JOURNEY

Standard Publishing
Cincinnati, Ohio

Project conceived, developed and edited by Dale Reeves
Assistant editor, Jim Eichenberger
Cover and inside design by Franke Design Company
Photo insert design by Sherry F. Willbrand
Photography by Jeff Frazier
AudioVision CD produced by Tedd T.   Additional producers: Bill Deaton, Mark Townsend.
Executive producers: Dan R. Brock, Eddie DeGarmo

Teen contributors: Rachel Eichenberger, Mandie Fields, Bethany Frederick, Andrea Harris, Melissa Harris, Bethany Stortz

Library of Congress Cataloging-in-Publication Data
St. James, Rebecca.
    40 days with God : a devotional journey / Rebecca St. James.
      p. cm.
    "Empowered Youth Products."
    ISBN 0-7847-0569-0
    1. Youth—Prayer-books and devotions—English. 2. Devotional calendars. 3. St. James, Rebecca. I. Title.
    BV4850.S7 1996
    242'.63—dc20   96-21810
                                                                                                        CIP
                                                                                                        AC

Published in association with the literary agency of Alive Communications, Inc. 1465 Kelly Johnson Blvd., Suite 320, Colorado Springs, CO, 80920

**The Standard Publishing Company, Cincinnati, Ohio
A Division of Standex International Corporation**

DEDICATION

To my dear great-grandma, Isabel Beasley, for the musical,
but more importantly, godly heritage you've passed on to me.
The stand you take for God at the age of 95 is an inspiration.
I love you.

To receive Rebecca's newsletter, write her at:
Rebecca St. James
P.O. Box 1741
Brentwood, TN 37024

Or, contact her by e-mail at her homepage address:
http://rsjames.com

Concert bookings: Ambassador
Tel: (615) 370-4700
Internet: 76135.3421@compuserve.com

ACKNOWLEDGEMENTS

"God"—that one word sums up everything: the reason I sing, who this is all about, the hope and purpose in my life, my greatest friend. I love You.

Dear friends:
I want to give a huge thanks to:
   • Mum, Dad and my whole family for the love, wisdom and life stories that have taught me so much and made this book possible!
   • Karleen and Kylie for being such great examples of true friendship. Love you both.
   • Dale, for everything . . . especially for your example, patience and for the countless hours, energy and hard work you have given.
   • Eddie, for your belief in us and in this ministry.
   • Ben Smallbone for your creative photography.
   • Wes Yoder and Rick Anderson for your support and especially your friendship.
   •The men and women who put together **Time With God,** the Bible devotional book that has helped me so much in my relationship with God.
   • The Standard team for your work and vision in reaching this generation with the hope—Jesus.
   • And thanks to you, the reader, for your love and support. Let's keep serving God together. Stay strong!

Your sister in Christ,

rebecca st.james

1 Corinthians 15:58

TABLE OF CONTENTS

FOREWORD

Welcome to **40 Days With God.** Our hope is that this book will give you a glimpse into the devotional life of Rebecca St. James. I have traveled on the road with Rebecca and her family and have seen firsthand how her intimacy with God is her strength and her inspiration. What you see on stage is genuine. With Rebecca, there is no pretense. She has opened herself up to God and has asked Him to direct her every step.

This devotional book was born out of several needs. When Rebecca's family moved to America a few years ago, they went through some very hard times. They quickly learned they had to depend on God's goodness in order to have their needs met. Prayer and Bible study as a family were crucial to their survival. They searched for a family devotional that they could use in their times of study. They didn't find much that seemed to be targeted to the whole family. Rebecca and her parents began to give some thought to the idea of writing their own devotional. I first encountered Rebecca's ministry in 1994 and was impressed with her passion for God at such a young age—then 16. This past year, I approached Rebecca about writing a book that would not only show us something of her relationship with God, but also challenge many others to grow along with her.

The way this book came together is evidence of God's working. Whenever "Bec" and I would begin to work on some of the content, she would always start by asking, "Do you want to pray first?" I have heard a number of her interviews in person and on the radio, and she always makes this request first. She really desires that what she says to others be God-directed, and not self-motivated. Quite a contrast to the culture in which we live today!

Over the course of several months I traveled with Rebecca and her family to get to the heart of what she had to say. We searched for just the right words for each entry, always asking God for His creativity and inspiration. I have seen a number of Rebecca's concerts and have witnessed how God is using her to minister to her peers, children and families in a dramatic way. I even became an honorary member of her family of nine, as we journeyed through the beautiful countryside of Vermont, New York and Pennsylvania for several days.

But this book is not just about her. It's about you. That's why we pulled together a group of six teenagers to help us write the "You Talk to God" sections. We wanted these devotions to be as practical as possible. It is our prayer that you will see much more than Rebecca, that you also will be challenged in your own spiritual walk with God. Read her stories and lyrics. Enjoy the photos and CD-ROM. But, if you really want to chronicle your spiritual growth, read all of the wisdom from God's Word, spend time with Him and talk to Him about what's on your heart. His Word has the power to change your life eternally.

Dale Reeves, editor

WHY 40 DAYS?

Does God care about numbers? As we read His Word, certain numbers "leap out" at us. God's leaders regularly appear in twelves—Jacob's sons, the spies scouting the riches of Canaan and the disciples of Jesus. When we notice God's mighty hand at work we find the number seven, as evidenced in creation and the conquest of Jericho. God speaks in threes—through the prophet, priest and king in the Old Testament and in His threefold Godhead—the Father, Son and Holy Spirit.

When our Father prepares His chosen for His work on earth, He repeatedly uses forty days to perform the task. We encourage the user of this journal to take a forty-day devotional journey with God. We need to escape from our pressures, schedules and distractions. We need to let Him prepare us for whatever use He has in mind. We need to allow new, God-honoring habits to take root in our lives. God's Word speaks of the fruit of some forty-day encounters with God.

Learning His word
When it was time to reveal the Law to the Israelites, Moses was equipped for the task. After forty days and nights with his Maker on Mount Sinai, he returned to his people with stone tablets of Law (Exodus 24:18). A forty-day trek is a great way to become grounded in our faith. God writes His Word on the tablets of our hearts.

Exploring His Blessings
As God's people approached the land of Canaan, twelve spies spent forty days scouting the blessings that lay in store for them (Numbers 13:25). In our fast-paced culture we often race past the gifts we are intended to enjoy. Forty days with God can allow us to sample the wealth of the land that lies before us.

Receiving His strength
On Mount Carmel, Elijah utterly defeated the prophets of Baal. But the showdown left him drained and depressed. Jehovah took His spokesman on a forty-day trip of renewal (1 Kings 19:8). Even the most mature believer is not invincible. Our daily struggles can leave us empty. Spending forty days with our Redeemer can take us off the battlefield, allowing us to be recharged by His still, small voice.

Following His will
Before embarking on His earthly mission, Our Savior was baptized by John and heard the voice of His Father, assuring Him of His Sonship. But His time of preparation was not complete until He spent forty days in the desert, committing His life to His mission (Matthew 4:2). Forty days in a quiet place with our God can cement our desire to give our all to His plans for us.

What will happen on your forty-day journey? We really do not know. But we encourage you to spend those days with the One who does.

PACKING INSTRUCTIONS

Are you ready to take off on your journey? You may not be traveling on a plane, train or automobile—you may not even leave your house—but you'd better be prepared for the ride of your life. Traveling God's way is a very exciting adventure indeed! You may choose to meet with your Father in the same place and at the same time every day. Or, you may decide to meet with Him at various locations and at different times. But, the important thing is to cultivate the habit of meeting with Him. Here are some tips to help you along the way.

plan the journey
Before you set out on a trip, you often talk to someone who has traveled to that destination before. You may even consult a guide. As you read the words of Rebecca, her journal entries and her song lyrics, you will see where she has been in her walk with God. Her insight and experience will help you plan and anticipate your encounter with God.

study the map
The Bible is God's road map for our daily lives. His words provide light for our journey. Approach the "God Talks" and "More Time With God" sections expecting God to speak to you personally. He will always steer you in the proper direction.

enjoy the ride
The journey is not meant to be mundane or tedious. Contrary to popular opinion, the Christian life is anything but boring. Jesus came that you might experience an exciting life. Each entry in this book provides an opportunity for you to talk to God. Communicate with Him as your best friend.

relive the adventure
You may wish to record the date you complete each of your journal entries. That way, when you come back and revisit this book in the future, you will see how far you have come in your journey with God. Commit to following His way, but be cautioned—this trip will be life-changing!

1

HOW "GOD" CAME ABOUT

 ## REBECCA TALKS

Often when I get out and take a walk, I notice many things around me, like a little flower. I might say, "Wow, that's God!" So many things happen in my life like that. Sometimes in my devotional times with God, I'll read something and it will just jump off the page at me, because it's exactly God speaking to me at that time. There's absolutely no other way to explain it—it's just Him! We are so small, and God is so huge! The fact that He thinks of us is just incredible! It just blows me away that He loves us so much.

Lyric from "god"

words by Rebecca St. James and Tedd T.
© 1996 Up In The Mix Music (A Division of The forefront communications group, INC.) (BMI)/Bibbitsong Music (Admin. by ICG) (BMI). All rights reserved. International copyright secured. Used by permission.

He made the night, He made the day; spread the earth upon the waters, Made the heavens and the rain.
Look at the sky, see its design; The very same creator is the one who gave us life.
And what is man that He's mindful of us? We're merely clay in His hands. And what am I that He loves me so much He would die? You know all I can say is . . .

It's God, truly God, can you see, can you hear, can you touch, can you feel?
It is God, truly God, I can't explain any other way 'cause it's God!

Inside us all there is a void; all mankind is searching for the one who fills the soul. In Him there's hope, in Him there's life. The world cries for a savior that's right before their eyes.
And what is man that He takes us in as His children to be His own? And what are we that He wants to be our Father? All that I can say is . . .

It's God, truly God, can you see, can you hear, can you touch, can you feel?
It is God, truly God, I can't explain any other way 'cause it's God!

Real amazing stuff happened when I went to Tedd's (my producer's) studio today. We prayed for God's strength and power because neither one of us had much sleep last night. Tedd had only slept three hours and I had just flown back from New Orleans, so we were both wiped. We talked about some verses God had given me and while we were praying, I got this idea. Why not write a song about "God" because I am always saying, "It's God!"? A melody had come into my head, so Tedd started a track. . . . By the end of that night, we had all of "God" finished except the bridge and second-verse lyrics! God is so good. When we are totally weak, He is totally strong. . . .

. . . Yesterday was another amazing day. In the morning we began at 9:00 A.M. since I've actually been getting up earlier lately! When we got to the studio Tedd wasn't there yet, so I got out some of my songs. Dad had commented the night before about how this world needs God. He had seen a recent **Newsweek** that spoke about the mental confusion of people. I immediately thought about this song. While sitting in the car, I thought about shaping the second verse to talk about the void inside everyone. That morning all these lines just kept coming to me. "God" was basically complete except for a little tweaking.

GOD TALKS

"O LORD, our Lord, how majestic is your name in all the earth!
You have set your glory above the heavens.
From the lips of children and infants you have ordained praise
Because of your enemies, to silence the foe and the avenger.
When I consider your heavens, the work of your fingers,
The moon and the stars, which you have set in place,
What is man that you are mindful of him,
The son of man that you care for him?"

PSALM 8:1-4, NIV

MORE TIME WITH GOD

Genesis 1:26, 31

Psalm 19:1-6

Psalm 29

Psalm 77:13-20

Psalm 90:2

YOU TALK TO GOD

✳ In what unique ways have I seen God's power through His creation?

✳ Have I ever felt a void in my life? When?

✳ What has God done in my life that I know could have come only from Him?

✳ God, thank You for demonstrating Your love for me in these ways . . .

2
YOU ARE WHAT YOU EAT

 REBECCA TALKS

I love to read the Bible. It is the coolest book. God's way is absolutely the only way. His Word is our instruction book. It's so practical. The Bible shows us where our priorities should be and how to live a happy and joyful life. I jot down verses that mean something to me in my journal. Sometimes, my producer, Tedd, and I will read the Word for five minutes, sometimes for half an hour or so. Then, we just pray and give it to God and ask Him for His creativity and His inspiration. Then He gives it to us and we give the glory to Him.

 REBECCA'S JOURNAL

Someone wrote to me and said, "Keep spending time with Jesus. I know it sometimes seems like there is no time, but make time to be with Him." That really challenged me. We are what we fill our minds with. If we're serious about becoming like Jesus, we must spend time with Him.

 GOD TALKS

"How well God must like you—you don't hang out at Sin Saloon, you don't slink along Dead-End Road, you don't go to Smart-Mouth College. Instead you thrill to God's Word, you chew on Scripture day and night."

PSALM 1:1, 2, THE MESSAGE

 more time with god

Joshua 1:8   Psalm 77:12   Psalm 119:17-24, 41-48   1 Peter 2:1-3

YOU TALK TO GOD

✳ My favorite foods are:

✳ What do I spend more time "chewing on" (thinking about) than anything else?

✳ What are some characteristics of God worth meditating on?

✳ Five of my favorite Scripture verses are . . .

1.

2.

3.

4.

5.

Help me, Lord, to commit these to memory, meditate on them and live by them.

awesome
aussie lingo
lollies = candy
chips = french fries
muesli = granola
porridge = oatmeal

3

EMPTY CUPBOARDS

REBECCA TALKS

There was a time in our family's life a few years ago that we had absolutely nothing. We had just moved to the U.S. and my Dad had lost his job. There were lots of empty cupboards and we weren't sure where the food was going to come from. My mum was pregnant with my sister and we didn't have any furniture in our house and didn't even own a car. We would just pray for our needs and God would provide cereal on our doorstep just when we needed it. (You don't know how quickly our family goes through cereal!) We saw so many miracles. It really taught us about trusting in God.

REBECCA'S JOURNAL

While I was waiting in Chicago for a delayed flight, an elderly lady walked by me, struggling to pull a bag and looking very confused. My heart tugged when I saw her, so I told God that if she walked by again, I'd ask her if she needed help. Well, she did. Then, I told God I would help if she sat down. After the woman found a seat, I said, "Okay, God, it looks like You might want me to do this. I'll do it if she stands up!" I finally worked up enough courage, went over and offered to help. I found out that she had been waiting over two hours for her family to pick her up. She needed help calling them. She was so grateful for my help that she actually wanted to pay me! I felt as though God was asking me, "Will you step out on the edge for Me, or will you be selfish and a slave to your fears?"

It is only when we get out of our comfort zones, and begin to live by faith, that we truly see God at work in and through our lives. Whenever I go on stage or do an interview, I pray, "Lord, just give me the words here. I can't do it without You." I always ask God to be with me and allow me to say what He wants me to. When I was writing lyrics for my second album, I had to trust God for His perfect timing.

 GOD TALKS

"If you want favor with both God and man, and a reputation for good judgment and common sense, then trust the Lord completely; don't ever trust yourself. In everything you do, put God first, and he will direct you and crown your efforts with success."

PROVERBS 3:4-6, TLB

 more time with god

Psalm 5:1-3
Isaiah 58:11
Matthew 6:8
Philippians 4:12, 13, 19

☎ YOU TALK TO GOD

✳ If God were to examine my degree of trust in Him, He would say . . .

✳ One time when I really trusted God to meet my needs was . . .

✳ How have I been guilty of trying to meet my own needs, rather than relying on God?

✳ How might God be calling me to leave my comfort zone?

4

FOLLOW THE LEADER

 ## REBECCA TALKS

A couple of my really big heroes are Mother Teresa and Billy Graham. Mother Teresa has such a servant's heart and looks at every single person and loves him like she would Jesus. I really appreciate Billy Graham for his integrity and his moral standards. If there's anybody I want to shape my life after, it's them. I look up to both of these people because they mirror Jesus.

REBECCA'S JOURNAL

I've been asked, "How would you like to be remembered?" I would love to be dubbed "a woman after God's own heart" because I long to have Jesus' attitude of servanthood and His love for the Father and others. But really, I'm just an 18-year-old wanting to be used by God in whatever way He wants, trying to live in His will.

 ## GOD TALKS

"Follow God's example in everything you do just as a much loved child imitates his father. Be full of love for others, following the example of Christ who loved you and gave himself to God as a sacrifice to take away your sins. And God was pleased, for Christ's love for you was like sweet perfume to him."

EPHESIANS 5:1, 2, TLB

MORE TIME WITH GOD

1 Corinthians 11:1

Hebrews 6:10-12

Hebrews 13:7, 8

YOU TALK TO GOD

✳ Two of the people I admire the most are:

1.

2.

✳ Do they project a Christlike image?

✳ Who are some positive role models that can guide me in imitating God?

✳ Some ways in which I would like to imitate God are . . .

5

SEARCH ME

REBECCA TALKS

On December 29, 1991, my little sister Elizabeth (otherwise known as Libby) was born. The amazing thing is that I got to watch the miracle of her birth. To see how God had created her so perfectly was just an indescribable moment in my life. Since then, I've had the opportunity to work with crisis pregnancy centers and really share from my own experience how God has a purpose for every baby formed in the womb.

Lyric from "psalm 139"

words by Rebecca St. James
used by permission.

You search me, You know me, You see my every move.
There's nothing I could ever do to hide myself from You. You know my thoughts, my fears and hurts, my weaknesses and pride.
You know what I am going through and how I feel inside.

But even though You know, You will always love me,
Even though You know, You'll never let me go.
I don't deserve Your love, but You give it freely.
You will always love me, even though You know.

REBECCA'S JOURNAL

Every now and then I receive a letter that breaks my heart. Here's an excerpt from one.

> "In your song 'True Love,' you talk about love that doesn't let you down. Yeah, right! How can you get that love? . . . I know that God loves me, but so what? Not like I can actually feel that love! . . . Thanks for at least reading this. I'll be praying for you. Keep up the good work for God. You know He loves it. I only wish He'd love me."

The fact that we are on this earth and were created by God shows how much He loves us. Every day, whether we decide to see it or not, God is offering His love, showing us His power through creation. He wants so much to spend time with us.

 ## GOD TALKS

"O LORD, you have searched me and you know me. You know when I sit and when I rise; you perceive my thoughts from afar. You discern my going out and my lying down; you are familiar with all my ways. Before a word is on my tongue you know it completely, O LORD. . . .

For you created my inmost being; you knit me together in my mother's womb. I praise you because I am fearfully and wonderfully made; your works are wonderful, I know that full well."

PSALM 139:1-4, 13, 14, NIV

 ### more time with god

1 Samuel 16:7

Psalm 103:13-18

Jeremiah 1:5

Matthew 10:29-31

YOU TALK TO GOD

* When I look in the mirror, I see . . .

* When my friends look at me, they see . . .

* When God looks at me, He sees . . .

Lord, I praise You for being the One who knows me the best and loves me the most.

awesome
aussie lingo
plait = braid

6

LIFE IS SHORT

REBECCA TALKS

In 1995 I came in contact with a guy named Wendall Kauffman through a "See You at the Pole" rally in a small town in Illinois. About nine months later, "Make a Wish Foundation" called to let me know he was dying of spinal cancer. They asked if I could see him before he died. I met with him for a few hours and saw how he was wasting away. I knew I would probably never see him again in this world. But when I looked into his eyes, I saw peace, because he knew exactly where he was going—to be with his best friend Jesus. It really taught me a lesson about how short this life really is. We need to make decisions now to get serious about God. We must use our lives for Him before it's too late.

REBECCA'S JOURNAL

Traveling home from my friend's house one night, I saw this sign on a church billboard: "Ten years from now, what will you wish you had done **now**?"

GOD TALKS

"So watch your step. Use your head. Make the most of every chance you get. These are desperate times!

Don't live carelessly, unthinkingly. Make sure you understand what the Master wants."

EPHESIANS 5:15-17, THE MESSAGE

 **more time with god**

Romans 13:8-14

James 4:13-17

1 Peter 1:22-25

 YOU TALK TO GOD

✳ What things keep me from using my time wisely?

✳ Ten years from now, what do I hope I will be able to say I've done?

✳ This week, I missed (or seized) an incredible opportunity to help someone else. It involved . . .

✳ I need Your help, Lord, disciplining my time to . . .

7
EVERYTHING I DO

REBECCA TALKS

A girl went to see a psychologist and was telling him all her problems. He said, "Why don't you stop doing what you're doing?" She responded, "You mean I don't have to do what I want to do?" She was enslaved to living life her way and giving in to her selfish desires. And it was ruining her life in the process. Selfishness does not pay. We need to get serious about the decisions we make each day because everything is a decision between God's way and our way.

Lyric from "Everything I Do"

words by Rebecca St. James and Connie Harrington © 1994 Up In The Mix Music/BMI/Bibbitsong Music/(admin. by Lori Kelly, Rights & Licenses)/BMI/Edward Grant, Inc. (ASCAP)/ admin. by Reunion Music, 2910 Poston Ave., Nashville, TN)/Nevertheless Music (admin. by Integrated Copyright Group)/ASCAP/All Rights Reserved. International copyright secured. Used by permission.

Everything I do, let it be in Your name, let it be for Your glory, let it be for You.
Everything I say, let it be in Your name, let it be to Your glory, let it be for Your sake
'cause I wanna please You in everything I do.

I want the world to see You when they look at me,
And I want the world to hear You in every word I speak. So let my words be Your words and my actions too, so they'll find the new life that I have found in You.

REBECCA'S JOURNAL

I wrote the chorus to this song while sitting outside in the sunshine (a favorite pastime of mine), just wanting to give God everything, every aspect of my life, all I do and say.

A prayer of mine—"Show me how to please You, dear God. May I be a light to this dark world. . . . Let me not think from a worldly perspective, but a godly one. I am Yours. Always."

 # GOD TALKS

"And whatever you do, whether in word or deed, do it all in the name of the Lord Jesus, giving thanks to God the Father through him."

COLOSSIANS 3:17, NIV

 m o r e   T i m e   w i t h   g o d

John 5:30

1 Corinthians 10:31-33

Galatians 6:7-10

Colossians 1:9-12

awesome aussie lingo
good on ya'= have a good day, well done, good job

☎ YOU TALK TO GOD

❋ What parts of my life do I have to admit I do for "my name," "my glory" and "for me"?

❋ On a scale of 1-10 (1 being self-centered and 10 being others-centered), where would I place myself?

1   2   3   4   5   6   7   8   9   10

❋ Lord, I come to You now to talk about my personal growth:

❋ Some aspects of my life You have already taken control of are . . .

❋ Some aspects of my life I need to let You take control of are . . .

8

GRANDMA'S STORY

 REBECCA TALKS

I love my great-grandmother. She is 95 and she is so cool. This past Christmas we were back in Australia and I got to see her. I asked her, "If you could say one thing to this whole generation, what would you say?" And she said, "We should not do anything that we would not want God to see." I thought that was some pretty serious accountability. She also said that life is like a car. There are certain things that you're not supposed to do, and things you're supposed to fill a car with, like oil and gas. In our lives, we're not supposed to do certain things, like have sex before marriage, and have drugs and alcohol inside our bodies—because they mess us up. Instead, we need to fill them with the Bible and things that are gonna help, like relationships that are gonna build us up, not tear us down. I think my grandmother has some pretty cool things to say.

 REBECCA'S JOURNAL

After a concert one night, I asked a youth minister what he had learned in his years of working with teens. He shared four things that our generation needs:

1. To hope in Jesus
2. To stop living for self
3. To have radical love for others
4. To love the unlovable

 GOD TALKS

"Finally, brothers, whatever is true, whatever is noble, whatever is right, whatever is pure, whatever is lovely, whatever is admirable—if anything is excellent or praiseworthy—think about such things."

PHILIPPIANS 4:8, NIV

more time with god

Psalm 15

Mark 7:14-23

Mark 12:28-31

Ephesians 5:15-18

 # YOU TALK TO GOD

✳ God, what is in my mind that You don't want in there?

✳ What kind of accountability do I have for my actions?

✳ What am I participating in that You would not want to see me doing?

✳ What am I doing that hurts You?

9

SIDE BY SIDE

 REBECCA TALKS

It is difficult to stand for God alone. We need people around us to keep us accountable, pray for us and encourage us to live sold-out for God. Imagine what would happen if we, as a generation, decided to unite and stand together side by side. We need friends in our lives that remind us about what is really important.

One of my best friends, Karleen, gives me serious accountability in my life. For instance, one night she came with me to one of my concerts. Right before it was about to start, she asked if I was nervous. And I said, "Yeah, a little bit." She said, "Just remember, it's all for God. All for God!" That's real friendship.

Lyric from "side by side"

words and music by bob farrell and eddie degarmo © 1994 dkb music/ascap/summerdawn music/ascap (administered by cmi) All Rights Reserved. International copyright secured. used by permission.

Everyday of my life, every valley I face,
    I know you'll always be there, every step that I take.
Let's keep our eyes on the father above,
    I need you, you need me, we need love.

side by side by side by side,
    walking together is the way it should be.
side by side by side by side,
    when you're needing somebody, depend upon me.
we'll travel on this journey of life side by side.

No need to go by yourself, or find the way on your own.
    You're never out of His sight, even when you're alone.
And I'll stay closer than a brother to you,
    Arm in arm, hand in hand, two by two.

side by side by side by side,
    walking together is the way it should be.
side by side by side by side,
    when you're needing somebody, depend upon me.
we'll travel on this journey of life side by side.

I was greatly encouraged when I received this letter from a 19-year-old guy in the Air Force. He writes,

> "Thanks for recording such a wonderful album. I listened to it almost all 16 hours of my flight over here. This is my first time away from home, which is over 6,000 miles away. I was really scared about coming here. My base is about 50 miles from North Korea. . . . I have felt alone because I didn't know anybody and I didn't have my parents around anymore. Your song 'Side By Side' comforted me and reminded me that I wasn't alone, and that God was with me. . .
>
> Ahn-nyong-hee kah-seh-yo (good-bye) from the land of the morning calm."

"I can do what you cannot; you can do what I cannot—together we can do something beautiful for God."—Malcolm Muggeridge

GOD TALKS

"Two can accomplish more than twice as much as one, for the results can be much better. If one falls, the other pulls him up; but if a man falls when he is alone, he's in trouble.

"Also, on a cold night, two under the same blanket gain warmth from each other, but how can one be warm alone? And one standing alone can be attacked and defeated, but two can stand back-to-back and conquer; three is even better, for a triple-braided cord is not easily broken."

ECCLESIASTES 4:9-12, TLB

M o r e   T i m e   w i t h   g o d

Psalm 133	John 17:21
Ephesians 4:1-6, 15, 16	Philippians 2:1-4

☎ YOU TALK TO GOD

✳ Recently, _____ (friend's name) helped me during this difficult situation:

✳ Some ways in which this person helped me make it through this trial are . . .

✳ Without this help, what might have happened to me?

✳ Lord, thank You for relationships in which I can be accountable and in which I can hold others accountable.

   Some people who hold me accountable are:

   Some people whom I can hold accountable are:

10

BE STRONG

REBECCA TALKS

I remember one time last year when I had three concerts in 27 hours. The worst part was that I was the sickest that I've been in a long time. I really had no voice, so I prayed that God would heal me. I walked out on stage and asked people to pray for me and ask God to work through the situation for all of us. I didn't get healed immediately, but my voice got progressively stronger as I sang. I felt broken, like I had nothing to give at all. Yet, this experience taught me that when we are weakest, God is strong.

REBECCA'S JOURNAL

I feel that God has been urging me to write a song on standing strong for Him without compromise because the verse "Be strong and courageous" has been popping up a lot. One thing I am learning about this country and our generation is that we're not standing for anything and that we desperately need to be standing for God.

GOD TALKS

"So let God work his will in you. Yell a loud **no** to the Devil and watch him scamper. Say a quiet **yes** to God and he'll be there in no time. Quit dabbling in sin. Purify your inner life. Quit playing the field. Hit bottom, and cry your eyes out. The fun and games are over. Get serious, really serious. Get down on your knees before the Master; it's the only way you'll get on your feet."

JAMES 4:7-10, THE MESSAGE

more Time with god

Joshua 1:6-9	1 Corinthians 15:58
Colossians 1:9-12	1 Peter 5:8-11

YOU TALK TO GOD

✳ God, help me recall my recent battles with the devil.
  ✳ A time I fought Satan and won:

Why did I win?

  ✳ A time I fought Satan and lost:

Why did I lose?

✳ Three areas of weakness in my life in which I need God's strength are . . .
  1.

  2.

  3.

✳ Father, I want You to work Your will in me
  when I face this situation today . . .

**awesome
aussie lingo**
fair dinkum =
serious, for real

11

GO AND SIN NO MORE

REBECCA TALKS

I was reading a part in the Bible where an adulterous woman came to Jesus. Actually, the Pharisees threw her down at Jesus' feet. They were convicting her of her sin. But Jesus is so cool. He says, "If anybody here hasn't sinned, then cast the first stone at her." And everybody walked away 'cause they had all sinned. And Jesus said, "Neither do I condemn you. Go and sin no more."

Lyric from "go and sin no more"

words by Rebecca St. James, Tedd T., and Michael Anderson © 1996 Up In The Mix Music (A Division of The Forefront Communications Group, Inc.) (BMI)/Bibbitsong Music (Admin. by ICG) (BMI). All rights reserved. International copyright secured. Used by permission.

I've sinned, come on my knees for I'm not worthy of your
    love. How could you die for me? such grace could only
come from God.
    oh, Lord, you search and you know me, you see me
inside out. God, you alone can forgive me, erase my fear
    and my doubt.
Father, you pick me up; I feel like a child in your arms.
    I don't deserve this love, but I hear your voice, Lord
Jesus.

"go and sin no more," He said, "I will not condemn you,
    I'll forgive and I'll forget it all."
"go and sin no more, my child, let me remind you it is I
    who'll lead and guide you as you go and sin no more."

wipe, wipe away; take, take away;
    break, break away;
fill my life, make it right;
    Father, help me, Father, help me go!

I've sinned, come on my knees, how could you die for
    me? you search my heart, know my thoughts, see me
inside out and all throughout me;
    you alone can forgive me, you always pick me up.
like a child in your arms, I could stay with you forever
    here.

I really believe that revival begins when we get on our faces broken before God, in total repentance realizing that we are nothing and He is everything. I'm sure the woman in John 8 realized she was empty, had nothing to give and that Jesus was her only hope. It is then that God can fill us and we can be used by Him.

GOD TALKS

"Then Jesus stood up again and said to her, 'Where are your accusers? Didn't even one of them condemn you?' 'No, sir,' she said. And Jesus said, 'Neither do I. Go and sin no more.'"

JOHN 8:10, 11, TLB

More Time with god

Psalm 51:1-7, 17

Psalm 103:8-12

Romans 8:1-4

James 5:16

1 John 1:8—2:2

awesome
aussie lingo
winge = to whine, cry

YOU TALK TO GOD

✳ I have always felt that God could never forgive me for . . .

✳ If others were to find out about this private sin, how would they treat me differently?

✳ A line from Rebecca's song that really speaks to me about God's forgiveness is . . .

✳ God, I need to respond to Your gift of forgiveness. Help me to "sin no more" in these areas of my life:

12

WHAT'S YOUR PURPOSE?

REBECCA TALKS

When I do a concert, often I like to start the evening by letting people know my purpose—that I hope it will be a worship experience, not just a show. I want it to be an encouragement to all of us to stand strong for God and to live a radical Christian life, supporting each other and relying on Him. God is my best friend in the world, the reason I sing, the reason I live and my total purpose for being.

second verse of "go and sin no more"

words by Rebecca St. James, Tedd T., and Michael Anderson © 1996 Up In The Mix Music (A Division of the Forefront Communications Group, Inc.) (BMI)/Bibbitsong Music (Admin. by ICG) (BMI). All rights reserved. International copyright secured. Used by permission.

You are my purpose, you are the reason that I live.
I want to be like you, help me to love and to forgive.
God, let me not be distracted; Lord, help me focus on
you. Keep sin from ruling my life, Lord, make me holy
and pure.
Father, you pick me up; I feel like a child in your
arms. I don't deserve this love, but, I hear your voice,
Lord Jesus.

REBECCA'S JOURNAL

We were created to live for God's purpose. We are sent into this world for such a time as this to be used by Him. We need to have a statement of purpose. We need to know what God wants us to do and begin now.

GOD TALKS

"It's in Christ that we find out who we are and what we are living for. Long before we first heard of Christ and got our hopes up, he had his eye on us, had designs on us for glorious living, part of the overall purpose he is working out in everything and everyone."

EPHESIANS 1:11, 12, THE MESSAGE

m o r e   t i m e   w i t h   g o d

Esther 4:14

Jeremiah 32:17-19

2 Timothy 1:8-10

YOU TALK TO GOD

* When I think about my friends, they are living for . . .

* When I think about myself, I am living for . . .

* If I were to summarize God's purpose for me, I would say . . .

* One way I can show God that I truly want to live for Him is . . .

13
PAIN?

REBECCA TALKS

A lot of people think that it must be pretty glamorous to be on the stage with the lights and the smoke and everything. But truthfully, it's hard for me to get up on stage in front of my peers and adults who have a lot more wisdom than me. And I really wish they could see me at six in the morning when I'm really tired!

Sometimes our attitudes aren't the best. But God has a way of showing us that through the fire, He makes us grow. I remember this one day I had been through a lot of hard stuff. In my devotional book that morning, the title was , "The Price of Following Jesus." It actually said, "Young lady, refuse to compromise." Pain teaches us things we can't learn any other way.

REBECCA'S JOURNAL

We are tested by fire for our own good. Philip Yancey has said, "Jesus' followers are not insulated from the tragedies of this world, just as He was not . . . rather . . . 'This suffering is all part of the work God has given you. Christ, who suffered for you, is your example. Follow in his steps.'" (1 Peter 2:21, TLB)

In Daniel 3:18, Shadrach, Meshach and Abednego told the king that "Even if He [God] doesn't!" deliver them from the furnace, they still would not bow to the king's statue of gold. Wow! What an uncompromising message! Even to the point of death, they were willing to pay the price for radically following God. God didn't deliver them from the furnace, but in the midst of it.

Could I say that to God—"Even if it costs me my life, I'll follow You!"? We must be so sure God is with us that we can say, "God, I want Your will at any cost to me!" Whether that means being laughed at, put down or misunderstood by people, we have to be faithful as God is to us. God desires unconditional commitment from this generation.

 ## GOD TALKS

"Consider it a sheer gift, friends, when tests and challenges come at you from all sides. You know that under pressure, your faith-life is forced into the open and shows its true colors . . . If you don't know what you're doing, pray to the Father. He loves to help. You'll get his help, and won't be condescended to when you ask for it. . . . Anyone who meets a testing challenge head-on and manages to stick it out is mighty fortunate. For such persons loyally in love with God, the reward is life and more life."

JAMES 1:2, 4, 12, THE MESSAGE

 more time with god

Acts 14:22

2 Corinthians 12:7-10

2 Timothy 2:3

1 Peter 4:12-19

awesome
aussie lingo
wog = sickness

YOU TALK TO GOD

✳ My attitude about hardship is . . .

✳ Have I ever been laughed at or put down because of my walk with Jesus?

✳ Am I willing to pay whatever price is necessary to be a true disciple of Jesus?

✳ A time when I was very weak, but God was strong within me was . . .

14

DON'T TAKE THEM FOR GRANTED

 REBECCA TALKS

I love my family. I have five younger brothers and one little sister. Whenever possible, all eight of them (including Mum and Dad) join me in a 15-passenger van and travel to my concerts that are nearby. I absolutely love it when they can be with me on the road. To them, I'm still just the same old "Bec." They treat me just like they always have, and there's great security in that. There's something about looking after your brothers and sister that really keeps you humble. You realize the stage doesn't mean anything. You set up, you sing, you try to minister and then it all comes back down and everyone goes home. My family helps keep me normal.

 REBECCA'S JOURNAL

A 15-year-old from Canada wrote and said,
"Give your dad a hug and tell him you love him,
for he won't be here on earth forever. It took the
death of my father for me to realize that."

 GOD TALKS

"Listen with respect to the father who raised you, and when your mother grows old, don't neglect her. Buy truth—don't sell it for love or money; buy wisdom, buy education, buy insight. Parents rejoice when their children turn out well; wise children become proud parents. So make your father happy! Make your mother proud!"

PROVERBS 23:22-25, THE MESSAGE

Proverbs 30:11-17

Galatians 6:7-10

1 John 4:19-21

 ## YOU TALK TO GOD

✳ What are some qualities about my parents that I really appreciate?

✳ Some lessons I've learned from my family are . . .

✳ What are some practical ways I can show my appreciation to my family?

✳ I plan to express my gratitude in the following ways this week . . .

awesome
aussie lingo
bloke = guy

15

CLEANING HOUSES

REBECCA TALKS

When we moved to the States a few years ago, God really opened up opportunities for our family to put food on the table. We would clean houses, and baby-sit and rake lawns as a family. It really taught me a lesson about servanthood. Life is about giving away, not taking all the time. We are called to serve others. Until we give ourselves away, we never truly discover what God wants from us. Whatever God has called us to be—whether it be a housecleaner, or a lawyer, a mailman, a missionary or whatever—that is our ministry.

Lyric from "Here I Am"

words by Rebecca St. James and Bill Deaton
© 1994 Up In The Mix Music/BMI/Bibbitsong
Music/(Admin. by Lori Kelly, Rights &
Licenses)/BMI/Queen Takes Pawn Music/
BMI/(Admin. by The Copyright Co., Nashville,
TN)/Dayspring Music (A division of Word,
Inc.)/BMI/All Rights Reserved. International
copyright secured. Used by permission.

God asks the question, "Whom shall I send?"
   Now, what will we answer?
Will we go and do as He says?
   All that He wants is a heart, ready, willing and waiting.

Here I am, I surrender my life to the use of Your plan.
   Here I am, I will do as You say; I will go where You send, Here I am.

REBECCA'S JOURNAL

Here I am in the Cook Islands. Yesterday I was sitting under the palm trees and prayed, asking God to speak to me. He led me to Philippians, and as I was reading familiar verses, I came across the part where Paul said, "I count everything as loss compared to the greatness of knowing Christ Jesus my Lord." I asked, "What am I to count as loss, God?" Things began to come into my head, and suddenly it was like a light turned on and I understood. A huge smile spread across my face because God had revealed this to me. Simple truth as it may be, I get real excited when God reveals anything to me. But this was real special because there is such freedom in knowing absolutely everything in life is loss compared to knowing my Jesus!

GOD TALKS

"What matters most to me is to finish what God started: the job the Master Jesus gave me of letting everyone I meet know all about this incredibly extravagant generosity of God."

ACTS 20:24, The Message

 more time with god

Matthew 16:24, 25

Matthew 23:11, 12

Luke 17:7-10

Luke 22:24-27

awesome
aussie lingo
serviette = napkin

YOU TALK TO GOD

❋ How does this world say I should make my way to the top?

❋ What does Jesus say?

❋ What is one way I can serve someone else today that will make a difference in his or her life?

❋ Whom is God calling me to serve in Jesus' name?

Someone at school?

At home?

Where else?

$\boxed{16}$
SACRIFICE

 ## REBECCA TALKS

A few years back, my dad went through a real humbling, growing time in his life. Through it he learned a lot about sacrifice. When we moved to the States, Dad had to leave his record company and business in Australia. Unfortunately, without him there, it fell apart. He had to let go of something he'd poured his soul into for fifteen years. One morning he was so down about it that he couldn't get out of bed. That same day, Eric Champion's father called and asked him to manage Eric. Through the pain of sacrifice, God had shown His power.

In August of 1993, my grandpa, who lived in Australia, was diagnosed with cancer. They operated on him and he seemed to be getting better. But, then he came down with pneumonia, and because he was so weak, he died. It was an extremely hard time for my family because we were on the other side of the world, and loved him so much. But, it was hardest on my dad, who couldn't be there to say good-bye to his father. Because of this pain, it made us really see that there is a cost involved in following God's will. Look closely at the credits of my first album and you'll see that it is dedicated to my grandpa for his unconditional love and likeness to Christ.

 ### REBECCA'S JOURNAL

Dudley Hall once said,
> "All of life is a trade. If you choose to follow
> God's will, you might miss out on some things,
> but what you gain will be much better."

I also read this quote once:
> "When we forget ourselves, we usually do
> something everyone else remembers."

 # GOD TALKS

"Then Peter chimed in, 'We left everything and followed you. What do we get out of it?' Jesus replied , 'Yes, you have followed me. . . . And not only you, but anyone who sacrifices home, family, fields—whatever—because of me will get it all back a hundred times over, not to mention the considerable bonus of eternal life.'"

MATTHEW 19:27, 29, The Message

 **More Time with God**

Luke 9:57-62   Luke 14:25-33   Philippians 2:12-18

 # YOU TALK TO GOD

* When I think about a time when I fell into a really good deal, I remember . . .

* The best bargain in life is trading what we think we want for what God knows we need. What things am I holding onto that I have been unwilling to lay down for God?

* What might happen if I chose to trade up for His deal?

* What might God be calling me to give up in order to really follow Him?

17

WHO'S IN CONTROL?

REBECCA TALKS

I never know how God might use a song to encourage someone. For example, I received this letter from a guy in Texas:

"During the time around your concert, God was doing a lot of things in my heart. He was telling me that my place was on the mission field. However, stepping out and totally turning myself over to His will was something that I wasn't really sure that I was ready to do.

". . . It was during your concert, while I was standing there with my hands high in the air and singing, 'Here I am, I surrender my life to the use of your plan' that I finally gave everything I had and everything I was to the Lord for Him to use. . . . Know that you are always more than welcome at my children's home in Belize, and that we will be praying for you without ceasing."

REBECCA'S JOURNAL

These are some of my favorite quotes on the subject of serving others:

"Die serving something greater than yourself."

"In serving each other we become free."

"Only a life lived for others is a life worthwhile."
—Albert Einstein

"There is joy in transcending self to serve others." —Mother Teresa of Calcutta

 **GOD TALKS**

"Whatever you do, work at it with all your heart, as working for the Lord, not for men, since you know that you will receive an inheritance from the Lord as a reward. It is the Lord Christ you are serving."

COLOSSIANS 3:23, 24, NIV

 more Time with god

Micah 6:6-8

Mark 10:42-45

John 15:9-14

Romans 12:9-13

 # YOU TALK TO GOD

✶ In my life, if God were a car part, He would be the . . .

❑ bumper   ❑ brake
❑ engine   ❑ spare tire
❑ steering wheel ❑ other _____

Why?

✶ The last time I did something for someone else was . . .

✶ My motivation for doing this was:

❑ my parents made me   ❑ my love for God
❑ my love for myself   ❑ I had no choice
❑ for recognition from others ❑ my love for others

✶ Lord, I ask You to take control in this area of my life . . .

18
GUARDING OUR MINDS

REBECCA TALKS

I really believe if we're going to be serious about living sold-out for God, we need to say, "I do **not** want to fill my mind with the junk that's out there. I don't want to waste my time putting things into my brain that I won't be able to get out." Lord, help us to be able to say, "If this is something You don't want me to see on TV or on a video, help me to turn it off. If this is something You don't want me to listen to on a CD, help me to throw it in the trash. Help me to spend time in Your Word that I might go against the grain and keep my mind **pure**."

REBECCA'S JOURNAL

On top of our television at home is a sign that serves as a great reminder to watch what we put into our minds. It says, "I will live with a pure heart in my own home. I will not put anything wicked before my eyes."
Psalm 101:2, 3

GOD TALKS

"And the peace of God, which transcends all understanding, will guard your hearts and your minds in Christ Jesus."

PHILIPPIANS 4:7, NIV

more time with god

Psalm 101:1-4   Psalm 119:9-16

Romans 8:5-9   Romans 12:1, 2

 YOU TALK TO GOD

❋ I can never get the song _____ out of my head.

❋ What anti-Christian images are ingrained in my thoughts concerning:
   ❶ sex?

   ❷ drugs and alcohol?

   ❸ celebrities?

   ❹ authority figures?

   ❺ God?

❋ What causes my mind to be filled with these misconceptions?

❋ I will take the following steps to clean up my mind . . .

awesome
aussie lingo
ice block = popsicle

19
YOU'RE THE VOICE

REBECCA TALKS

The first time I heard the song "You're the Voice" was when I was just a little kid in Australia. It was such a powerful song that many kids my age still remember it from their childhood. To me, it is a total call to our generation to not be silent, to not compromise. We are God's mouthpiece, His voice, to share with people the truth—that life is about living for Him and not living for ourselves.

The secular media (music, television, etc.) has really sold us a lie that life is about just doing what "feels good." Unfortunately, this generation has listened to that voice and accepted it as truth. But there is only one Truth. And He needs to be the voice that guides our lives.

The amazing thing is that God uses us, even as teenagers, to be His voice to a searching and confused generation. Maybe God is challenging you to start a Bible study with some friends or in your school. If He is, go for it in God's strength. Be His voice.

Lyric from "You're the voice"

words by M. Ryder, K. Reed, A. Quinta, and C. Thompson © 1986 Rondor Music (London Ltd.) Bluebeard Music Ltd. (PRS) and C.T. Music Ltd. All rights reserved. Used by permission.

we have the chance to turn the pages over. we can write
    what we want to write, we gotta make ends meet
before we get much older.
    we're all someone's daughter, we're all someone's
son; How long can we look at each other down the barrel
    of a gun?

you're the voice, try and understand it. make a noise and
    make it clear. we're not gonna sit in silence, we're not
gonna live with fear.

This time you know we all can stand together. with the
    power to be powerful, believing, we can make it better.
we're all someone's daughter, we're all someone's son;
    How long can we look at each other down the barrel
of a gun?

A 15-year-old girl from Orlando, Florida wrote, "Your challenge to join or start a Bible study has really moved me to action. I am now a part of a club at our school called Frontline. We meet every morning to pray, share our problems and concerns and study the Bible. We also have outreaches every Tuesday and Thursday after school. . . . I can see that our world is in need. I look around me, not even very far, and I see people so full of desperation. They're longing for meaning and purpose, but they're searching in all the wrong places. Many may never realize that the one place where they can find true peace is the very place they are running from. . . . I see now, more than ever before, youth who are standing up for righteousness, truth and integrity— not only in word, but also in deed."

GOD TALKS

"Does not wisdom call out? Does not understanding raise her voice? . . . Listen, for I have worthy things to say; I open my lips to speak what is right."

PROVERBS 8:1, 6, NIV

More Time with God

Psalm 40:8-10

Ezekiel 3:17-19

Acts 4:13-20

2 Timothy 1:7, 8

YOU TALK TO GOD

✳ If I had fifteen minutes on TV to be the "voice of truth" to my culture, I would say . . .

✳ So, I'm not on TV, but my voice can still be heard in the following places, by the following people:

✳ Here are three ways I can make my voice heard to these people:

1.

2.

3.

✳ Lord, I want to be the "voice of truth." During the next month, I will take the following steps to accomplish one of the goals listed above:

awesome
aussie lingo
news agency = a shop
that sells newspapers,
magazines and office
supplies

$\boxed{20}$

WHY DO I BELIEVE?

REBECCA TALKS

At a Girls' Brigade meeting when I was eight years old, I gave my life total-ly over to God. I still vividly remember coming home afterwards and crying my little eyes out. My mum had written down in a book that I'd said, "It makes me cry when I realize how much Jesus loves me." And, still to this day, it amazes me that He loves us so much He would die for us! That night changed my life. It's the best decision I've ever made!

REBECCA'S JOURNAL

A self-proclaimed agnostic from Canada once asked me, "Would you be willing to die for your beliefs? Would you die for your God?" In a very honest (but sad) letter, she wrote,
> "Christianity is not worth my time or effort. I'm an agnostic on my way to becoming an atheist. As deeply as you believe in God, is as deeply as I don't believe. I cannot love your God. My heart does not long for eternal or spiritual things. I have no use for heaven or eternal life, when all I want is my physical and emotional pain to end now. I want happiness on earth, while I'm alive. . . .
>
> "God does not exist in my world. When I suffer, I suffer alone. There is no one who looks from above. If there is a God who does see, he laughs when I am reeling with pain, and trips me when I just get up from a bad fall."

How tragic! I would love to sit down and talk with her about how much God really does love us and how He proves that to me every day! I've seen miracles, and more importantly, felt Him working inside of me, giving me hope and purpose. I've seen Him totally rearrange others' lives. Would I be willing to die for my God? The answer is Yes!

"Until we find a cause worth dying for, we're not really living."—Ron Luce

 ## GOD TALKS

"Then he [Jesus] focused his attention on Thomas. 'Take your finger and examine my hands. Take your hand and stick it in my side. Don't be unbelieving. Believe.'

"Thomas said, 'My Master! My God!'

"Jesus said, 'So, you believe because you've seen with your own eyes. Even better blessings are in store for those who believe without seeing.'

"Jesus provided far more God-revealing signs than are written down in this book. These are written down so you will believe that Jesus is the Messiah, the Son of God, and in the act of believing, have real and eternal life in the way he personally revealed it."

JOHN 20:27-31, THE MESSAGE

 more time with god

John 4:39-42

John 9:35-38

John 14:9-14

1 Corinthians 15:1-6

YOU TALK TO GOD

✺ If I were a detective whose job was to prove the existence of a loving God, I would present the following case:

❶ Circumstantial Evidence
Here's how I see God's presence in the natural world:

❷ Sworn Testimony
Here's some impressive evidence from the Bible:

❸ Reliable Witnesses
Here's how I see God working in the lives of others:

❹ Firsthand Evidence
Here's how God has recently worked in my life:

awesome
aussie lingo
streuth = wow, that's
incredible!

21
SPEAK TO ME

REBECCA TALKS

Recently I got together with a friend and told him about this verse I'd found that said, "Speak to me, for your servant is listening." Around the same time, he played this chord progression for me on his guitar. He said it soothed him and, when I heard it, I understood why. As he was playing, I started singing this chorus to it and God just brought it together. He totally gave us the song, "Speak to Me."

In order to hear God's voice, we must get into the Bible, and talk with Him daily, so that we can truly know Him. One of the things God has challenged me to do more is to just be still and sit at His feet. No agenda. No particular requests. Just time spent with my Father.

Lyric from "speak to me"

words by Rebecca St. James, Josh Deaton, and Tedd T.
© 1996 Up In The Mix Music (A Division of The Forefront Communications Group, Inc.) (BMI)/Bibbitsong Music (admin. by ICG) (BMI)/Queen Takes Pawn Music (BMI) (admin. by The Copyright Co.) All rights reserved. International copyright secured. Used by permission.

speak to me, Lord, for your child is here listening.
speak to me, Lord, for your child is here waiting on you. speak to me, Lord, for your child is here listening.
speak to me, Lord, for your child is here waiting on you. unveil my eyes, let me see, see you.
unveil my heart, let me know, know you, father do.

you are the true god, the one living Lord, father.
you are the true god, the one living Lord, father you.
you are the true god, the one living Lord, father.
you are the true god, the one living Lord, father you.

Jesus, your word stands forever, changing me forever.
speak to me, Lord, for your child is here listening.
speak to me, Lord, for your child is here waiting on you.

I don't remember who said it, but I really believe it: "It is in your time with God that He will prepare and equip you to serve Him. . . . One will naturally serve God out of one's time spent with Him. . . . Spending time with God is the first step to serving Him."

GOD TALKS

"Now Samuel did not yet know the LORD: The word of the LORD had not yet been revealed to him. . . . The LORD came and stood there, calling as at the other times, 'Samuel! Samuel!' Then Samuel said, 'Speak, for your servant is listening.' . . . The LORD continued to appear at Shiloh, and there he revealed himself to Samuel through his word."

1 SAMUEL 3:7, 10, 21, NIV

 More Time with god

Ecclesiastes 12:11-13

Luke 10:38-42

John 6:66-69

John 10:2-4, 14-16

awesome
aussie lingo
g'day = Hello or
what's up?

YOU TALK TO GOD

✳ The individual I'm closest to is _____.
On the average, I spend about this much time with this friend every day:

In person   _____

On the phone   _____

Just thinking about this friend   _____

Total time each day   _____

✳ What other activities do I give up to spend time with this person?

✳ On the average, I spend about this much time with God every day:

In prayer   _____

In Bible study   _____

Talking about Him with others   _____

Total time each day   _____

✳ What can I give up in order to spend more time to hear God's voice?

With my brothers Daniel and Ben. Behind us is one of Australia's panoramic views!

"All-dressed-up" for Girls' Brigade. It was at one of these meetings that I gave my life to God.

Horseback riding—one of my secret loves—at age 6.

Daniel, Joel, Ben and me in costume for a trip to Old Sydney Town.

A step back in time!

Looking a little younger . . .

(l-r) Libby, me, Joel, Daniel, Luke, Josh and Ben.

This isn't the "Sound of Music"

but there are 7 of us! (l-r) Luke (9), Elizabeth (4), Daniel (16), me (18), Joel (11), Joshua (6) and Ben (14).

Dale Reeves

Wendall Kauffman and me, a few months before he passed away.

Thanks to Make a Wish Foundation for allowing us to meet.

Hangin' out with "radio guys" Lee and Roger

in Houston at KSBJ.

Together on the road—Mum, Dad and me—good friends!

A dramatic moment
in concert. That's my
brother running lights.
(I'm a proud sister!)

Ben Smallbone

Dale Reeves

Reading out of THE
MESSAGE . . . "Get

serious, really serious.
Get down on your
knees before the
Master.

It's the only way
you'll get on
your feet."
James 4:10

With some kids in
New Mexico, shooting
a video for Compassion
International.

Compassion International

We can stand together—The
Side by Side Tour.

Above
all
things . . .

Daniel 3 . . .
The vision.

Dale and me—the
devotional writing team!
This photo was taken
on the road, putting
this book together.

On a mission trip to
Ecuador with Teen
Mania. I became friends
with this little girl. After
giving her some clips

for her hair, I told her
"Jesus loves you" in
Spanish. We bonded!

Teen Mania

Hangin' out with the
band (l-r) Brent
Milligan, Vince
Emmett, Tom Laune
(engineer), me,
Tedd (my fabulous
producer!) and Dan
Needham.

ForeFront Communications

Mother and daughter—
backstage at the
Dove Awards.

"You want
me to sign your
water
bottle?"

True Love Waits—
Atlanta Georgia Dome.
344,000 purity pledges
go Thru the Roof!

Jeff Frazier

I loooove this photo!
My little sister Libby and me.

22

"I WANT TO BE LIKE YOU!"

REBECCA TALKS

When we spend time with someone, we are influenced by that person and often tend to act like him or her. As we spend time with God, and listen and obey Him, we are changed. Our goal is to become more and more like Jesus every day.

I just read something really cool out of THE MESSAGE: "The fear of human opinion disables; trusting in God protects you from that" (Proverbs 29:25). This really speaks to us, because our generation is constantly concerned with what others **think**, rather than what God **says**—and we are falling morally because of it. But if we learn to trust God, then we're worried only about what **He** thinks of us—and that's the only way to live!

REBECCA'S JOURNAL

"speak to me"

words by Rebecca St. James, Josh Deaton, and Tedd T. © 1996 Up In The Mix Music (A Division of The Forefront Communications Group, Inc.) (BMI)/Bibbitsong Music (Admin. by ICG) (BMI)/Queen Takes Pawn Music (BMI) (Admin. by The Copyright Co.) All rights reserved. International copyright secured. Used by permission.

Jesus, your word stands forever, changing me forever.
speak to me, Lord, for your child is here listening.
speak to me, Lord, for your child is here waiting on you.

GOD TALKS

"And we know that all that happens to us is working for our good if we love God and are fitting into his plans. For from the very beginning God decided that those who came to him—and all along he knew who would—should become like his Son, so that his Son would be the First, with many brothers."

ROMANS 8:28, 29, TLB

more time with god

John 3:30

1 Corinthians 15:45-49

2 Corinthians 3:12-18

Colossians 3:5-10

1 John 3:1-3

 ## YOU TALK TO GOD

✳ Growing up, people said I always acted like _____ (a member of my family) because . . .

✳ I have become a lot like _____ (one of my friends) in these ways:

✳ In my walk with God, I have become more like Him in these ways:

✳ Lord, may You change me to be more like You in these ways:

awesome aussie lingo
oi = "hey," a way to attract attention

23

YOU DON'T DATE?

REBECCA TALKS

I've watched some of my friends date, then break up. It's so painful. I don't want that kind of pressure. I just want to stick with friendships with guys my age. When I eventually start dating, it will only be with guys I know I could possibly marry. It's in God's hands. For now, my choice is group dating. You can be yourself and have a bunch of fun. I love being friends with guys and doing fun stuff—like playing outdoor games or hiking.

I wear a promise ring to remind myself of the commitment I've made to God and my future husband, the choice to not have sex until after I'm married.

REBECCA'S JOURNAL

One day as I was thinking about the subject, I wrote this letter to my future husband:

My dear husband,

I love you already. My heart will be foremost God's and then yours. I eagerly await what God has in store for us. It is so great that we will have Him as the center and strength of our marriage and our lives. I am praying for you, knowing that you are waiting for me, as I am you. I pray that God will teach both you and me the things He wants us to learn before we meet.

Yours truly, Rebecca

GOD TALKS

"'For I know the plans I have for you,' declares the LORD, 'plans to prosper you and not to harm you, plans to give you hope and a future. Then you will call upon me and come and pray to me, and I will listen to you. You will seek me and find me when you seek me with all your heart.'"

JEREMIAH 29:11-13, NIV

more time with god

Psalm 37:3-7

Proverbs 16:3

Proverbs 19:21

 ## YOU TALK TO GOD

✷ As a child growing up, what were some of my dreams for the future? My future education?

My future career?

My future spouse and family?

✷ When I think about my goals in these areas now . . .

✷ The hardest dream for me to give up would be . . .

Lord, I place my future in Your hands. I know that if Your will does not match my dreams, You will provide something even better. Help me to trust in You.

awesome
aussie lingo
wagging = skipping
school or work;
being lazy

24
NO WORRIES

REBECCA TALKS

As a kid, I used to worry about things a lot (and still do, at times). I remember Dad would come and talk me through it. We would pray together and I'd end up laughing about it. After a bookstore appearance recently, someone reminded me of the verse in the Bible where it says not to worry, that God clothes even the flowers of the field and He loves us much more than them. I really needed to hear that. Sometimes we tend to take the problems of the world on our shoulders when all we need to do is trust God and realize that in Him we really have "no worries."

REBECCA'S JOURNAL

One of my favorite videos (mostly because it's Australian) is a ballroom dancing movie called "Strictly Ballroom." The major quote and theme of the movie is, "A life lived in fear is a life half-lived."

Someone once said,

"Worry is a burden God never meant for us to bear."

GOD TALKS

"People who don't know God and the way he works fuss over these things, but you know both God and how he works. Steep your life in God-reality, God-initiative, God-provisions. Don't worry about missing out. You'll find all your everyday human concerns will be met.

"Give your entire attention to what God is doing right now, and don't get worked up about what may or may not happen tomorrow. God will help you deal with whatever hard things come up when the time comes."

MATTHEW 6:32-34, THE MESSAGE

MORE TIME WITH GOD

Matthew 6:25-34	Matthew 11:28-30
John 14:12-14	Philippians 4:6
1 Peter 5:6, 7	

YOU TALK TO GOD

✳ My top five worries are . . .

1.

2.

3.

4.

5.

✳ In what ways are my worries keeping me from enjoying life?

✳ If my worst possible fear came true, what would happen to me?

✳ How would God be with me even in the midst of that situation?

Lord, thank You that Your love and concern for me are far greater than any of my worries.

awesome
aussie lingo
no worries = no
problem

25

WORSHIP

 ## REBECCA TALKS

I grew up in a home where praise music was very much a part of our lives. I attended my first Christian concert when I was six weeks old. "Above All Things" is very special song to me because I love to praise God. It's also a concert favorite of mine, because I love helping others worship Him.

 ## REBECCA'S JOURNAL

Lyric from "Above All Things"

words and music by Eddie DeGarmo
© 1994 DKB Music/ASCAP/All Rights
Reserved. International copyright
secured. Used by permission.

I cannot tell you all the reasons why Jesus, in His
    wisdom, took an interest in my life.
It must be endless, the boundaries of His grace,
    for He is patient with us, and worthy to be praised.

For above all things He is powerful,
    And above all things He is the King,
And above all things He is merciful,
    For above all things He thought of me.

I can't conceive it, the torture of the cross,
    The Author of creation gave us life at His own cost.
And all those present thought the grave would be
    the end,
But Jesus rose above it, and so will I, my friend.

For above all things He is powerful,
    And above all things He is the King,
And above all things He is merciful,
    For above all things He thought of me.

 # GOD TALKS

"'Ah, Sovereign LORD, you have made the heavens and the earth by your great power and outstretched arm. Nothing is too hard for you. You show love to thousands but bring the punishment for the fathers' sins into the laps of their children after them. O great and powerful God, whose name is the LORD Almighty, great are your purposes and mighty are your deeds.'"

JEREMIAH 32:17-19, NIV

 ## More Time with God

John 4:23, 24

Hebrews 13:15, 16

1 Timothy 1:15-17

Revelation 15:2-4

Revelation 19:11-16

YOU TALK TO GOD

✳ It has been said, "We become like that which we worship."
The things I worship or think about most are . . .

✳ Someone once said, "Don't tell me what's important to you. Let me see
your calendar and your checkbook and I'll tell you what's important."
This past week I have spent my time and my money on . . .

✳ To really worship God above all things, I need to . . .

✳ God, You are worthy to be praised today and forever because . . .

26

CELEBRATE HIM!

 ## REBECCA TALKS

Our youth group at my church in Franklin, Tennessee decided to make up a dance routine to the track "Joyful, Joyful We Adore Thee" from the movie **Sister Act 2.** It was so cool to sing this song (actually some of the guys rapped it) and worship God while we danced. There were about thirty of us and it was amazing to see how God unified us as we celebrated Him.

 REBECCA'S JOURNAL

Mother Teresa was asked to give a job description for coming to work with her in grimy Calcutta. Without hesitation she said one would need two things—the desire to work hard and a joyful attitude.

 ## GOD TALKS

"Celebrate God all day, every day. I mean, **revel** in him!"

PHILIPPIANS 4:4, THE MESSAGE

 more time with god

Nehemiah 12:27, 43

Psalm 98:4-6

Psalm 100

Psalm 145:3-7

YOU TALK TO GOD

Lord, I want my life to be filled with celebration.
If my life were a party and You were the guest of honor . . .

✳ Some food I would serve would include:

✳ Some people I would want to invite are:

✳ A gift I would bring to You would be:

✳ I song I would sing to You would be:

awesome
aussie lingo
sunnies = sunglasses,
shades

27

ME WITHOUT YOU

REBECCA TALKS

I pray before everything. Sometimes it's very intimidating to get up on stage before adults and before my peers. Praying to God is really my strength. I just have to look at Him and say, "You have it totally under control. You're a great God! It's Yours to do with as You see fit. You take it!" Prayer is so powerful. Without God, we are absolutely nothing.

REBECCA'S JOURNAL

Lyric from "Me without you"

words by Martin Briley
© 1995 Martin Briley Music/
ASCAP/All Rights Reserved.
Used by permission.

Like a band without a drummer, that's me without you.
    Like a year without a summer, that's me without you.
Like a king without a country, like a room without a
    view, like an empty gun, like a fatherless son, that's
me without you.

Like a ship without a rudder, that's me without you.
    Like a child without its mother, that's me without
you. Like a story with no ending, like a foot without a
    shoe, like a wasted feast, like a faithless priest,
that's me without you.

Me without you, a pitiful sight,
    Me without you, it ain't never gonna feel right.

Like a war without an enemy, that's me without you.
    A disease without a remedy, that's me without you.
Like a crime without a victim, like a sleuth without a
clue, like an empty gun, like a fatherless son, that's me
without you.

Me without you, a pitiful sight,
    Me without you, it ain't never gonna feel right.

 # GOD TALKS

"Now to him who is able to do immeasurably more than all we ask or imagine, according to his power that is at work within us, to him be glory in the church and in Christ Jesus throughout all generations, for ever and ever! Amen."

EPHESIANS 3:20, 21, NIV

 More Time with God

Psalm 62:5-8

Matthew 7:7-11

John 15:1-5

1 John 5:13-15

awesome
aussie lingo
petrol = gasoline

YOU TALK TO GOD

When Rebecca says that without God she's like a "ship without a rudder," she means that she would have no direction without His leading. Take a look at those lyrics again. Now, it's your turn.

✳ I'm like a _____ without a _____, which means I rely on God for . . .

✳ I'm like a _____ without a _____, which means . . .

✳ A time when I needed guts to do something for God was . . .

✳ How has He been my Rock, providing strength and confidence?

✳ God, You are my Rock, You are my Fortress. Without You I can do nothing. I thank You for . . .

28

I'M MEANT TO BE PERFECT?

 REBECCA TALKS

When I was in Australia last year, I visited some friends who live on twelve and a half thousand acres. I was sitting next to a lake, praying, "God, what can I do to go further with You?" I felt like He clearly said to me, "Just look around you. See this beautiful earth—the clouds, the trees, the water, the sunset, everything. What do you see?" I said, "God, it's so perfect!" Then I felt as though He said, "Be perfect as I am perfect." I must be content with nothing less than holiness. That's what I should strive for.

 REBECCA'S JOURNAL

On a wall in my room, I have these ten reminders:
1. Stay strong in the faith
2. Be content with what you have
3. Do your best always
4. Help others before you help yourself
5. Be God-conscious
6. Be thankful
7. Let the Lord shine through your life
8. Be an example of perseverance and love
9. Have Christ's attitude
10. Don't forget to count your blessings!

I might not live by all of these every day, but they're worthy goals to strive for. Everybody is watching to see what's going to happen with this generation. This is where Christians come in and say, "Jesus is the answer"—lived out through us.

 GOD TALKS

"Be perfect, therefore, as your heavenly Father is perfect."

MATTHEW 5:48, NIV

m o r e   T i m e   w i t h   g o d

Ephesians 1:4

Colossians 1:21, 22

1 Timothy 6:6

1 Peter 1:15, 16

 # YOU TALK TO GOD

✷ What personal spiritual goals have I set for myself this year?

✷ What can I do better tomorrow than I did today?

✷ God, help me to be more like Jesus in the following ways . . .

29

WHAT CAN I DO?

REBECCA TALKS

Remember when you were a kid and people asked you, "What are you going to do when you grow up?" Well, I really don't believe that we have to be "grown up" to be used by God. God is God, and He can use whomever He wants—no matter how young. I think as teenagers we need to be using these years to do God's will and make a difference. We are part of a generation He is calling to be sold-out for Him.

In Australia, only five percent of the population attends church, and being a Christian often draws a lot of negative attention. It's really black-and-white. If you're a believer in Jesus, people ask why you go to church.

God may be calling you to serve Him outside your country, or He may just want you to serve your friends and neighbors right where you live. He may call you to go on a foreign mission trip, or just a daily mission trip in your neighborhood. The important thing is to bloom where you're planted.

REBECCA'S JOURNAL

Last summer my brother Daniel and I had the chance to go on a mission trip. We sensed real unity in Ecuador with Teen Mania. We made a lot of great friends. We handed out tracts saying "Jesus te ama" ("Jesus loves you" in Spanish). I really pray that God planted many seeds through that. Daniel and I also shared our testimony. I sang and played the part of a pregnant lady in a skit! We prayed in the huddles. We spent lots of quality time at the little restaurants around Cuenca with quality people. It was so cool to see teens on fire for God and making a difference.

GOD TALKS

"Jesus went through all the towns and villages, teaching in their synagogues, preaching the good news of the kingdom and healing every disease and sickness. When he saw the crowds, he had compassion on them, because they were harassed and helpless, like sheep without a shepherd. Then he said to his disciples, 'The harvest is plentiful but the workers are few. Ask the Lord of the harvest, therefore, to send out workers into his harvest field.'"

MATTHEW 9:35-38, NIV

 ## more time with god

Isaiah 6:8

Matthew 28:16-20

John 4:34-36

Acts 1:8

Romans 10:13-15

awesome
aussie lingo
chemist = pharmacist

☎ YOU TALK TO GOD

✸ How are my friends "harassed and helpless, like sheep without a shepherd"?

✸ How does God want me to be a worker for Him among my friends?

✸ How might God want me to serve Him ten years from now?

✸ How should I be preparing for that goal right now?

✸ Is God calling me to share the gospel somewhere I've never considered?

$\boxed{30}$
SET AN EXAMPLE

REBECCA TALKS

I am the oldest of seven children and I absolutely love it! But with the fun also comes responsibility. I want to be a big sister they can look up to who is an example of Jesus to them. But for any of us to do this, we've got to set high standards, keep in the Bible and prayer—and be kept accountable. A good accountability check is to ask, in all of your activities, "How far does this take me away from prayer and focusing on God?" "How far does this take me from the activity of loving my neighbor and treating people sensitively?"

REBECCA'S JOURNAL

I remember the day when I met a woman who was in the New Age movement. She thought all Christians were hypocrites. I told her, "Please don't judge Christ by Christians, because a lot of times we're not a very good example of who He is." This lady had never heard anyone say that before!

St. Francis of Assisi said, "In all that you do, be a witness, and if necessary, use words." Our generation is looking to see if we're walking our talk.

GOD TALKS

"Don't let anyone put you down because you're young. Teach believers with your life: by word, by demeanor, by love, by faith, by integrity."

1 TIMOTHY 4:12, THE MESSAGE

More Time with God

Matthew 5:13-16

Colossians 4:5, 6

1 Peter 2:11, 12

 # YOU TALK TO GOD

Lord, help me to teach believers with my lifestyle:

❋ **by word**

something I need to say but haven't . . .

❋ **by demeanor**

an attitude I need to change . . .

❋ **by love**

someone whose needs I should put before my own . . .

❋ **by faith**

a risk I need to take because I know that it's Your will . . .

❋ **by integrity**

an area in my life in which I haven't been totally honest . . .

31

TRUE LOVE

REBECCA TALKS

It was totally cool to be a part of the "Thru the Roof" rally in the Georgia Dome last February. Over 10,000 teenagers attended, and saw over 344,000 abstinence commitment cards hoisted to the top of the stadium—20 stories high! The cards came from all over the U.S. and over 75 countries. The first stack of cards made it to the top, and a second stack reached five stories high. Today's teens are under a lot of pressure and are being forced to make a lot of big decisions early in life—especially when it comes to sexuality. I am a virgin, and I'm proud of it. I've made that commitment to God and to my future husband—whoever that may be.

God knows us totally—inside and out—and He understands the sexual struggles we face. He created sex. But He wants us to wait for when it's really right—marriage. But, if you've already been involved sexually, don't give up. In Christ you can be totally forgiven. You can be a recycled virgin.

Lyric from "True Love"

words by Tom Douglas and Johnny Christopher © 1982 saddleshoe publishing/bmi/easy nine/bmi/all rights reserved. international copyright secured. used by permission.

True love, talking 'bout true love, gotta have real (god's) love. whatcha gonna do? True love.

Love don't hate, love don't play those games with your mind. Love forgives and true love lives forever and all time. I'll never treat you like a stranger, turn my back in times of danger; love don't act that way, I said love don't act that way.

True love, talking 'bout true love, gotta have real (god's) love. whatcha gonna do? True love.

Love is patient, love is kind, love won't let you down; it won't deceive, love will never keep the past around. Never worries, never lies, no, it never leaves you, never dies. Love don't act that way, I said love don't act that way.

I received this letter from a guy who lives in Germany: "I was so glad to hear you want to wait 'til you're older to date; and only with people who you'd think of marrying. That's so important! I have remained sexually pure and am proud, like you, that my spouse will be able to experience my faithfulness, and never have to give me more than just who she is. . . . Like God can't stand any other gods before him, neither should my future wife have to stand for anything less than my entire devotion. My affection and faithfulness for her has already begun. It's funny that some think it's only after you're married that you've got to be faithful. . . . It's nice knowing you and others like you are out there, standing up for what is pure and holy."

 ## GOD TALKS

"Since we want to become spiritually one with the Master, we must not pursue the kind of sex that avoids commitment and intimacy, leaving us more lonely than ever—the kind of sex that can never 'become one.' There is a sense in which sexual sins are different from all others. In sexual sin we violate the sacredness of our own bodies, these bodies that were made for God-given and God-modeled love, for 'becoming one' with another. Or didn't you realize that your body is a sacred place, the place of the Holy Spirit? Don't you see that you can't live however you please, squandering what God paid such a high price for? The physical part of you is not some piece of property belonging to the spiritual part of you. God owns the whole works. So let people see God in and through your body."

1 CORINTHIANS 6:17-20, THE MESSAGE

Proverbs 6:20-29   1 Corinthians 10:12, 13

Galatians 5:19-21   1 Thessalonians 4:3-8

YOU TALK TO GOD

✳ The world's idea of "true love" (safe sex) is . . .

✳ A lot of teenagers follow this idea instead of God's way because . . .

✳ I can remain sexually pure by committing to the following:
   Things I need to avoid . . .

   Things I need to do . . .

   Things I need to say . . .

   The way I dress . . .

If I have already messed up, I will not give up. God, please forgive me and help me to glorify You with my body.

32

FRIENDS—WHAT WOULD WE DO WITHOUT THEM?

 REBECCA TALKS

In the eighth grade, I began writing the song "Little Bit O' Love." It was inspired by my little brother Joel after I found him crying at school one day. I gave him a hug and some encouragement and he ran off and was happy again. For weeks afterward, he wanted to hang out with his "big sister." It taught me that a little bit of love truly does go a long, long way.

Later, that same year, I had to write a jingle for a music assignment— with my friends Kylie, Alison and Deanna. Our product was a washing detergent. The jingle was easy . . . "A little bit o' Beam put in your machine! Just a little bit o' Beam, it'll make your clothes real clean! Just a little bit o' Beam!" (I think we got an "A"!)

 REBECCA'S JOURNAL

I received a letter of encouragement from my cousin, Claire Bonner. Actually, she's not just my cousin—she's a friend of mine, too! She said, "I'm sure you realize that sometimes in doing lots of things for God, we begin to run out of time for God. It's a tactic of the enemy—he convinces us that we need to fill up our lives with this, that and the other when really there isn't anything better for us than to slow down and love God. 'Be still and know that I am God.'"

 GOD TALKS

"'You are my friends when you do the things I command you. I'm no longer calling you servants because servants don't understand what their master is thinking and planning. No, I've named you friends because I've let you in on everything I've heard from the Father.'

"'You didn't choose me, remember; I chose you, and put you in the world to bear fruit, fruit that won't spoil. As fruit bearers, whatever you ask the Father in relation to me, he gives you.'"

JOHN 15:14-16, THE MESSAGE

Proverbs 18:24   James 2:21-24   James 4:4-6

 YOU TALK TO GOD

✳ My best friend is _____.

✳ The qualities I appreciate most in this person are . . .

✳ A time recently when my friend encouraged me was . . .

✳ How has this person helped me mature in Christ?

Lord, thanks for my friends and the way they care for me. Help me to develop a closer friendship with You.

awesome
aussie lingo
mate = friend, buddy

33

WE DON'T NEED IT!

 REBECCA TALKS

We don't need "stuff" to be happy—the perfect body, or the best-looking car, the most up-to-date clothes, or the best house on the best street. We need Jesus Christ to be our total priority and not let that other stuff get in the way. I think this is the key to happiness. For when we admit that we don't need worldly riches and instead, rely on God, we've got a lot less to worry about and life becomes simpler and more enjoyable.

Lyric from "we Don't Need It"

words by Rebecca St. James and Bill Deaton © 1994 up in the mix music/BMI/Bibbitsong music (Admin. by Lori Kelly, Rights and Licenses)/BMI/Queen Takes Pawn music/BMI/(Admin. by the copyright co., Nashville, TN)/BMI/Blair Masters music/BMI/All rights reserved. International copyright secured. used by permission.

You can have the money, wheel it, deal it, win it all.
  You can have all of the fashion; you can even own the mall. You can change your face into the person of your
  dreams, trim your nose and dye your hair and change your eyes from blue to green. You can be a
  model, cover every magazine. You can walk on every stage or be the host of MTV. You can win the medals, run
  it, swim it perfectly. You could have a turn at Indy; you could even own the team.

we're never gonna see god if we keep looking for vogue;
  we could gain the whole world but still be losin' our soul.

we don't need it, 'cause god has given us our needs,
  we don't want it. shouldn't He be our priority?
we don't need it; Jesus said to leave it all behind.
  Let's keep our eyes on things above 'cause
we don't need to want to need it!

You can get a job on wall street, have more money than
  you've seen. You can buy administrations and you can even own the queen. You can own a castle, oily
  paintings on the wall, build a suite for every pleasure, have a disco, host a ball; drive a Lambourghini, fast as
  time and painted red, leather phone and matching fax and color TVs overhead. Take your yacht to Rio, fly
  your jet up to Cancun, screamin' down the highway like a rocket to the moon.

R E B E C C A ' S   J O U R N A L

The media says, "Life is a game. He who dies with the most toys wins." But that's just not true. I love the T-shirt that says, "He who dies with the most toys still dies."

GOD TALKS

"But all these things that I once thought very worthwhile—now I've thrown them all away so that I can put my trust and hope in Christ alone. Yes, everything else is worthless when compared with the priceless gain of knowing Christ Jesus my Lord. I have put aside all else, counting it worth less than nothing, in order that I can have Christ."

PHILIPPIANS 3:7, 8, TLB

m o r e   t i m e   w i t h   g o d

Proverbs 23:4, 5

Matthew 6:19-24

Matthew 19:16-26

Luke 12:15-21

**awesome
aussie lingo**
jumper = sweater
trolley = cart

YOU TALK TO GOD

✳ Two years ago, something I just had to have was . . .

✳ How important is it today? Has it lost its value to me?

✳ What other treasures that I value today will probably end up being tomorrow's trash?

✳ All I really need is Jesus. I will demonstrate that He is my priority by . . .

34

A NO-SECRETS KINDA FAMILY

REBECCA TALKS

One of the things that's really helped our family life is our "no secrets" policy. We have made a commitment to do things together. When we were going through our "living by faith" experience, Mum and Dad would tell us about every desperate financial and physical need and share with us exactly what was going on. When God provided for our needs, we knew exactly how incredible those miracles were. Even when we lived in Australia and Dad was promoting concerts, we would all go, even staying at the auditorium until two in the morning, just to be together.

Now, we home-school and travel as much as we can as a family. That has allowed us to become friends. We talk about everything and especially spiritual matters. Our family is a team.

REBECCA'S JOURNAL

I love having a big family. There is always someone to talk to, play with, laugh with. I hope to have seven or ten of my own children one day, God willing and my future husband willing. I am almost like a second mother to a lot of the kids, except for my eldest brother, who is taller than me!

GOD TALKS

"There should be no division in the body, but that its parts should have equal concern for each other. If one part suffers, every part suffers with it; if one part is honored, every part rejoices with it."

1 CORINTHIANS 12:25, 26, NIV

more time with god

Joshua 24:15-18

Ephesians 6:1-3

2 Timothy 1:3-5

YOU TALK TO GOD

✳ In what ways has my family shown me more about God?

✳ Some things my parents have taught me are . . .

✳ Someone who has been a "second mom" to me is_____.

✳ Ways she has helped me spiritually or emotionally include . . .

✳ God, You have revealed more of Your character to me through my family (or second mom). Thank You. Help me to show my appreciation by . . .

awesome
aussie lingo
dill = being silly

35

DON'T BOW!

REBECCA TALKS

In Daniel 3 everyone was bowing down to a statue of gold—everybody except three guys. I had a vision about our generation and what God is calling us to be. The world is bowing down to the gods of money, drugs, alcohol, MTV and selfishness. But God is calling us to be the Shadrachs, Meshachs and Abednegos of this generation. We don't have to bow down to the gods of this world. While the rest of the world is bowing, we can stand apart and be different.

Lyric from "carry me High"

words by Rebecca St. James and Tedd T. © 1996 Up in the Mix Music (a division of the Forefront communications Group, Inc.) (BMI)/Bibbitsong Music (admin. by ICG) (BMI). all rights reserved. International copyright secured. used by permission.

They laugh 'cause they see I live for more than me.
   They point their fingers, push me nearer to the flame.
They say, "we serve no one, we just live to please
   ourselves." All men serve something.

Father, carry me high, lift me to the sky,
   Let me be where you are.
Hold me, ever so closely, let me know your mercy;
   Let me be where you are.

They can laugh, but let them see you are the hope in me.
   They can point their fingers, push me nearer to the
flame. God, you can save me from the fire. I'm yours,
   even if you don't. whatever comes, I take this vow, I
will never bow.

Until you find something worth dying for, you're not
   really living. I will never bow.

Father, carry me high, lift me to the sky,
   Let me be where you are. I want to be where you are.
I will never bow.

This song was a total miracle. I was sitting on a plane. (And you know how noisy planes are.) I wasn't thinking about anything. I was just looking out the window at the clouds. I think we were flying into Cincinnati. This song, which is actually a prayer, just started singing itself in my brain. The words just kept coming and coming. It was such a "God thing." I recorded it on my little tape recorder as soon as we got to the airport!

GOD TALKS

"Shadrach, Meschach, and Abednego replied, 'O Nebuchadnezzar, we are not worried about what will happen to us. If we are thrown into the flaming furnace, our God is able to deliver us; and he will deliver us out of your hand, Your Majesty. But if he doesn't, please understand, sir, that even then we will never under any circumstance serve your gods or worship the golden statue you have erected.'"

DANIEL 3:16-18, TLB

m o r e   t i m e   w i t h   g o d

Exodus 20:1-6

Psalm 40:6-8

Psalm 135:15-18

Isaiah 44:9-19

awesome
aussie lingo
lift = an elevator

YOU TALK TO GOD

❋ When I look at others my age, I see them bowing down to . . .

❋ Lord, I thank You that You have delivered me from the appeal of these gods:

1.

2.

3.

❋ The idols that still tempt me the most are . . .

❋ Father, help me to not place my trust in these other "gods." I desire to do Your will in the following ways . . .

36

THE HARD TIMES

REBECCA TALKS

The Bible tells us not only to expect suffering to come, but to consider it a gift when it does come. And we are to be joyful in the midst of it. Chuck Swindoll defines joy as "living above the circumstances." That means that our happiness does not depend on how things are going, but on God's constant goodness—even when things are hard. God has really been teaching us as a family how to be content, whatever the circumstances.

REBECCA'S JOURNAL

In the movie, **Shadowlands**, C. S. Lewis said that the pain in our lives is like God chipping away at us like we're made out of stone or marble. Even though it hurts, He's making us into the person that He wants us to be. He's molding and defining us. I think that's exciting!

GOD TALKS

"I've learned by now to be quite content whatever my circumstances. I'm just as happy with little as with much, with much as with little. I've found the recipe for being happy whether full or hungry, hands full or hands empty. Whatever I have, wherever I am, I can make it through anything in the One who makes me who I am."

PHILIPPIANS 4:11-13, THE MESSAGE

more time with god

Acts 5:40, 41	Romans 5:3-5	Philippians 3:10, 11
	Hebrews 12:7-11	Revelation 2:2, 3

YOU TALK TO GOD

✴ When's the last time I actually thanked God for the suffering that came my way?

✴ When have I been disciplined by the Lord and didn't understand why?

✴ What was He trying to teach me?

✴ When it comes to the subject of contentment in my life, where would I place myself on this line?

1	2	3	4	5
(Very content)				(Very unhappy)

God, help me understand more about this "No pain—No gain" principle of the Christian life.

awesome
aussie lingo
shamozzle = chaos,
a disaster

37

HUNGRY FOR GOD?

REBECCA TALKS

One of the real priorities in my life is time with God, especially time spent reading the Bible. There are so many things that totally hit me over the head and are right where I am. I remember one time I was really worried about something and the headline for that day's devotion was "Trust God Completely." I love it when things like that happen and God makes verses jump off the pages at me.

Sometimes keeping a daily time to read the Bible is hard, but I think it is very important to be disciplined about getting into the Word, because it's feeding us with wisdom for life.

REBECCA'S JOURNAL

A teenager in Memphis wrote,
"I enjoy your music because in each song, each message is different, yet has the same foundation, Jesus Christ. . . . I'm asking if you could send me a few Bible verses that you turn to when you feel unsure, or confused. . . . What do I do to build my faith and have a more solid relationship with God?"

She's got it. The Bible is what we turn to when we don't understand things in life, and it is how we build our faith and get to know God.

 **GOD TALKS**

"Nothing is perfect except your words. Oh, how I love them. I think about them all day long. They make me wiser than my enemies, because they are my constant guide. Yes, wiser than my teachers, for I am ever thinking of your rules. They make me even wiser than the aged.

"I have refused to walk the paths of evil for I will remain obedient to your Word. No, I haven't turned away from what you taught me; your words are sweeter than honey."

PSALM 119:96-103, TLB

 more time with god

Psalm 34:8-10

Isaiah 55:1, 2

Matthew 5:6

Hebrews 5:13, 14

awesome aussie lingo

vegemite = a brown salty substance that americans liken to asphalt! (actually, it's a spread that people put on bread or toast, as popular in australia as peanut butter is in the u.s.)

tucker = food

cutlery = silverware

YOU TALK TO GOD

❋ My favorite fast-food restaurant is . . .

❋ When I think of a person who has fed me spiritually, I think of . . .

❋ How has this individual helped me create a solid relationship with God?

❋ Some of the reasons I don't spend more time in God's Word are . . .

❋ This week I will show my hunger for God's Word by . . .

38
GIVING HOPE

 REBECCA TALKS

A couple of years ago I visited a Zuni Indian reservation in New Mexico for Compassion International. It was rather eye-opening. I never knew that kind of poverty existed in America. I saw this one wall that had "Death" written on it in graffiti. Every day these people live with problems such as drugs, alcohol and suicide. But when I visited the Compassion school, the difference was like night and day. Those kids had Jesus. They had hope and a reason to live. We can be a part of changing the cycle by sponsoring children like these and reaching out to lonely people around us. We could be the only Jesus they will ever see.

 REBECCA'S JOURNAL

David Mata was awarded "Outstanding Young Person of the World" in medical science. While speaking at a graduation ceremony, he asked, "What will you do that will make an impact on the world? What will you do that will make a difference in the lives of others for eternity? If you will not work to serve your fellow man, what will you do? The greatest gift that we can give to this world is a life lived for Jesus."

 GOD TALKS

"The Christian who is pure and without fault, from God the Father's point of view, is the one who takes care of orphans and widows, and who remains true to the Lord—not soiled and dirtied by his contacts with the world."

JAMES 1:27, TLB

m o r e   T i m e   w i t h   g o d

Matthew 6:1-4   Matthew 25:31-46   1 John 3:16-18

YOU TALK TO GOD

✳ When was the last time I did something for someone else without being asked?

✳ Do I serve others so that I will be noticed or do I serve them in secret?

✳ Five specific things I could do to show my love for widows or orphans are:

   1.

   2.

   3.

   4.

   5.

✳ I plan to do the following . . .

by (date)_____.

39

MAKE IT COUNT

 R E B E C C A   T A L K S

People often ask me if I always wanted to be a singer. And truly, it was never a big dream of mine. It was one of those things that God directed. He took it one step at a time and made it happen when **He** wanted it to happen. Looking back, I see the seasons I've gone through in my life. And there were lessons to be learned in each of them.

On my second album is a song called "That's What Matters." Based on the book of Ecclesiastes, the chorus says:

> "Don't wish for a better day. Be glad and use the one you're in. Fear God and do exactly what He says. That's what matters. All else fades like the flowers."

 R E B E C C A ' S   J O U R N A L

TAKE TIME

Take time to think; it is the source of power.
Take time to read; it is the foundation of wisdom.
Take time to play; it is the secret of staying young.
Take time to be quiet; it is the opportunity to seek God.
Take time to be aware; it is the opportunity to help others.
Take time to love and be loved; it is God's greatest gift.
Take time to laugh; it is the music of the soul.
Take time to be friendly; it is the road to happiness.
Take time to dream; it is what the future is made of.
Take time to pray; it is the greatest gift on earth.
—author unknown

GOD TALKS

"There is a right time for everything:

    A time to be born, a time to die;

        A time to plant; a time to harvest;

    A time to kill; a time to heal;

        A time to destroy; a time to rebuild;

    A time to cry; a time to laugh;

        A time to grieve; a time to dance;

    A time for scattering stones; a time for gathering stones;

        A time to hug; a time not to hug;

    A time to find; a time to lose;

        A time for keeping; a time for throwing away;

    A time to tear; a time to repair;

        A time to be quiet; a time to speak up;

    A time for loving; a time for hating;

        A time for war; a time for peace.

What does one really get from hard work? I have thought about this in connection with all the various kinds of work God has given to mankind. Everything is appropriate in its own time. But though God has planted eternity in the hearts of men, even so, man cannot see the whole scope of God's work from beginning to end."

ECCLESIASTES 3:1-11, TLB

 m o r e T i m e w i t h g o d

Psalm 39:4, 5

Ecclesiastes 8:5, 6

Hosea 10:12

awesome
aussie lingo
fortnight = two weeks

☎ YOU TALK TO GOD

✸ Sometimes I have days that seem meaningless. I remember a day like that when . . .

✸ God says that He has a purpose for every day I live. What might He have been trying to teach me that day?

✸ I am impatient. I want God to take control of my life, but I want results NOW! While I am waiting for God's timing, I need to take time to . . . (Rebecca's journal has some ideas to get me started.)

40

GOD-CONSCIOUS

REBECCA TALKS

I always used to wonder what the Bible meant when it said, "Pray continually." It seemed like an impossible command to me. Then I really felt God saying that I was to be God-conscious at all times, to always have that line open to Him. It's so easy just to focus on ourselves and take our eyes off God. Many people today are into immediate gratification and are always wanting to be entertained. But the most joyful people are those who forget self. God is calling us to be more God-conscious than self-conscious.

REBECCA'S JOURNAL

"When you are more Father-conscious than people-conscious, more than things-conscious and self-conscious—you've got your secret [inside] life in order."   —Dudley Hall

"The people that God uses and chooses, God's all-stars, are not people of ability; they are people of availability who have learned the secret of giving their praise to God. If you use your life for the glory of God, God will use your life for His glory."
—James Merritt

GOD TALKS

"Be joyful always; pray continually; give thanks in all circumstances, for this is God's will for you in Christ Jesus."

1 THESSALONIANS 5:16-18, NIV

m o r e   t i m e   w i t h   g o d

Deuteronomy 6:4, 5

2 Chronicles 7:14

Luke 18:1-8

Colossians 4:2

 YOU TALK TO GOD

✱ **I am on trial to determine if I am self-conscious or God-conscious.**

❶ When I testify that I am God-conscious, I will say:

❷ As "proof" of my personal time with God, I will say that one of the best places for me to talk to Him is . . .

❸ If God were to show a video of my behavior, how would it contradict my testimony?

✱ One way in which I am trying to be less selfish is . . .

awesome
aussie lingo
jolly well = a word of
emphasis, stronger
than "very"

CD-ROM INFORMATION

Hidden on this AudioVision CD are artist interviews, full-length videos and much more. To try the disc, you'll need at least an MPC ll Windows or Mac 040 computer with 5 MB available RAM and a 2x CD-ROM drive. Because Enhanced CD technology is brand-new, these minimum configurations can't guarantee that the disc will perform on every system, but most computers will play the disc, and we hope yours is one of them.

On a Windows Machine
1) Ensure Windows is running. 2) Access the file manager. 3) Double-click the RSJ CDROM drive.
4) Double-click on README.txt.

On a Macintosh
1) Double-click the CDROM icon on your desktop. 2) Double-click on README (MAC).

Attention: Please read the important instructions inside before playing this AUDIOVISION CD. You have purchased the latest innovation in multimedia software, the Ardent AudioVision CD. This disc contains music, interviews, videos and more. It contains both standard CD audio and computer data files. A small percentage of CD audio players not manufactured to proper specifications may attempt to play the computer data as music. This could be both unpleasant and potentially damaging to your stereo system if you don't take the following precautions the first time you play your AVCD.

1. Turn the volume all the way down on your stereo system.
2. Press "play" on your CD player.
3. Slowly bring up the volume. If you hear any static-like noise, use the skip forward controls on your CD player to advance to the next track.
4. If you still encounter problems, as an AVCD customer, ForeFront Comm. has arranged for you to receive FREE introductory membership to CompuServe: Just dial 1-800-524-3388 and ask for representative 548.

(If you don't encounter any noise or other problems during the above procedure, it will not be necessary to repeat the process on subsequent plays.) Due to the high demands of interactive multimedia CD-ROM software and the large number of different computer configurations, the smooth operation of each particular configuration cannot be guaranteed.

SOFTWARE LICENSE AGREEMENT
Please read this license carefully before using the software. By using the software, you are agreeing to be bound by the terms of this license. If you do not agree to the terms of this license, then you must agree to not insert the AudioVision CD into a personal computer's CD drive.

1. LICENSE   The application, demonstration, system and other software contained on this CD (the "Software") and the related documentation and other materials ("Materials") are licensed to you by Ardent Records ("Ardent"). You own the CD on which the Software and Materials are recorded, but Ardent and/or Ardent's licensors retains title to the Software and Materials. This license allows you to use the Software and Materials on a single computer. You agree not to use the Software and Materials for any purpose other than personal use for entertainment.

2. RESTRICTIONS   The Software and Materials contain copyrighted materials, trade secrets and other proprietary materials. In order to protect them and except as permitted by applicable legislation, you may not decompile, reverse engineer, disassemble or otherwise reduce the Software to a human perceivable form. You may not modify, network, rent, lease, loan, distribute or create derivative works based upon the Software and Materials in whole or in part. You may not electronically transmit the Software and Materials from one computer to another or over a network.

3. TERMINATION   This License is effective until terminated. You may terminate this license at any time by destroying the CD Software and Materials and all copies thereof. This License will terminate immediately without notice from Ardent if you fail to comply with any provision of the License. Upon termination, you must destroy the Software and Materials and all copies.

4. EXPORT LAW ASSURANCES   You agree and certify that neither the Software nor any other technical data received from Ardent, nor the direct production thereof, will be exported or re-exported outside the United States except as authorized and as permitted by the laws and regulations of the United States and the jurisdiction in which you obtained the Software.

5. LIMITED WARRANTY ON MEDIA   Ardent warrants that CDs on which the Software and Materials are recorded are free from defects in materials and workmanship under normal use for a limited duration to ninety (90) days from the date of delivery. Ardent's entire liability and your exclusive remedy will be replacement of the CD which is returned to Ardent or an authorized Ardent representative with a copy of the receipt. Ardent will have no responsibility to replace a CD damaged by accident, abuse or misapplication. ANY IMPLIED WARRANTIES ON THE CD, INCLUDING THE IMPLIED WARRANTIES OF MERCHANTIBILITY AND FITNESS FOR A PARTICULAR PURPOSE, ARE LIMITED IN DURATION TO NINETY (90) DAYS FROM THE DATE OF DELIVERY. THIS WARRANTY GIVES YOU SPECIFIC LEGAL RIGHTS, AND YOU MAY ALSO HAVE OTHER RIGHTS WHICH VARY BY JURISDICTION.

6. DISCLAIMER OF WARRANTY ON SOFTWARE   You expressly acknowledge and agree that the use of the Software and Materials is at your sole risk. The Software and Materials are provided "AS IS" and without warranty of any kind. Ardent and Ardent's Licensor(s) (for the purposes of provisions 6 and 7, Ardent and Ardent's Licensor(s) shall be collectively referred to as "Ardent") expressly disclaim all warranties, express or implied, including but not limited to, the implied warranties of merchantibility and fitness for a particular purpose. Ardent does not warrant that the functions contained in the Software will meet your requirements, or that the operation of the Software will be uninterrupted or error-free, or that defects in the Software will be corrected. Furthermore, Ardent does not warrant or make any representations regarding the use or the results of the use of the Software and Materials in terms of correctness, accuracy, reliability or otherwise. No oral or written information or advice given by Ardent (or an Ardent authorized representative) assume the entire costs of all necessary servicing, repair or correction. Some jurisdictions do not allow the exclusion of implied warranties, so the above exclusion may not apply to you.

7. LIMITATION OF LIABILITY   The liability of Ardent for a breech of a condition or warranty in this agreement is limited to any one or more of the following (at Ardent's option): (1) replacement of the goods or the supply of equivalent goods; (2) the payment of the cost of replacing the goods or of acquiring the equivalent good. Under no circumstances, including negligence, shall Ardent be liable for any incidental, special or consequential damages that result from the use or inability to use the Software and Materials even if Ardent or an Ardent authorized representative has been advised of the possibility of such damages.

8. CONTROLLING LAW AND SEVERABILITY   In respect of any Apple Software, this license shall be governed by and construed under the laws of the USA and the State of California, as applied to agreements entered into and to be performed entirely within California, between California residents; and in respect of any Ardent Software this License shall be governed by and construed in accordance with the laws of the USA and the state of Tennessee. If for any reason a court of competent jurisdiction finds any provision of this license, or portion thereof, to be unenforceable, that provision of the license shall be enforced to the maximum extent permissible so as to effect the intent of the parties, and the remainder of this License shall continue in full force and effect.

9. COMPLETE AGREEMENT   This license constitutes the entire agreement between the parties with respect to the use of the Software and Materials and supersedes all other understandings or agreements, written or oral, regarding such subject matter. No amendment to or modification of this License will be binding unless agreed in writing and signed by a duly authorized representative of Ardent.